About the Book

Flash! Lightning zigzags across the sky. Crash! Thunder roars from the clouds. The wind blows and rain pours down.

A storm can be both a fascinating and a frightening experience. Understanding what makes a storm with thunder and lightning, what causes rain, sleet, hail, and snow, and how to keep safe during a storm are explored and explained by Melvin Berger in a way that will stimulate boys and girls to ask questions and encourage them to use their own observation.

Fine illustrations by Joseph Cellini add to the drama and understanding of the subject.

Each book in the *Science Is What and Why* series has been checked for scientific accuracy by an expert.

STORMS

by MELVIN BERGER

Illustrated by
JOSEPH CELLINI

Coward-McCann, Inc.   New York

General Editor: Margaret Farrington Bartlett
Consultant: Theodore D. Johnson
Montclair Public Schools

STORMS

Flash!
Lightning zigzags across the sky.
Crash!
Thunder roars from the clouds.
Dark clouds hide the sun.
Strong gusts of wind
blow dust and dirt all around.
Suddenly rain pours down.

"A thunderstorm!" someone shouts.
People rush to get out of the rain.
Drivers put on their car lights
because it is getting dark.
The rain makes little rivers
that flow down the street.
Lightning lights up the sky like a giant flash bulb.
Thunder follows, roaring like a hundred cannons.
You run into your house to watch the excitement.
It's fun to watch a storm—from indoors!

After a while the thunder and lightning stop.
Rain stops falling, and the sky clears.
The winds are still.
The air is fresh and clean.
"Where did the storm come from?" you ask.
"Where did it go?"

Most thunderstorms begin on hot summer afternoons.
The summer sun warms the air.
And the sun warms the earth.
Heat from the earth warms the air even more.

The air over some places is warmer
than the air over other places.
Factories, cars, and buildings give off heat.

12

This makes the air over cities warmer
than air over the country.

More of the sun's heat bounces up into the air
from land than from water.

This makes the air over land
warmer than the air over water.
How high up the air is
is also important.
Air over valleys is usually warmer
than the air over mountains.

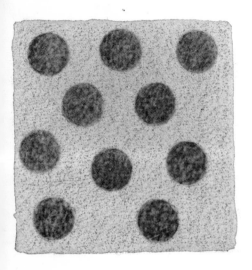 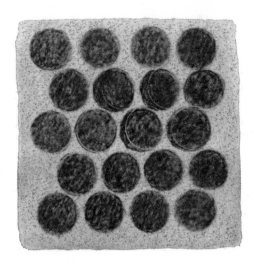

All air is made of tiny bits,
called *molecules*.
When air is warmed,
the molecules move farther apart.
There are big spaces between the molecules of warm air.
This makes warm air very light.
The molecules of cool air are packed tightly together.
This makes cool air heavier than warm air.

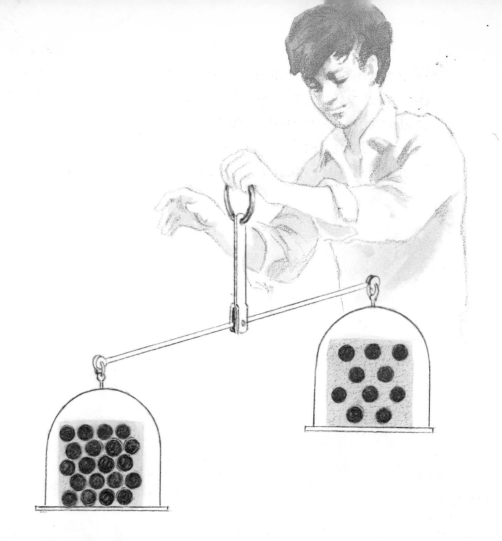

Imagine two jars of the same size.
One is filled with cool air,
and the other is filled with warm air.
More air molecules fit into the jar with cool air,
since they are closer together.
The jar with the cool air is heavier
than the jar full of the warm air.
Cool air is heavier than the same amount of warm air.

When warm air meets cool air,
the heavy cool air pushes in
under the light warm air.
The cool air pushes the warm air up.
It makes the warm air rise.

As the warm air rises,
cool air rushes in.
This rushing of air is a wind.
You can create a wind in your house.
Close the door to the bathroom
and run hot water into the tub.
The hot water heats the air in the bathroom.
Open the door a crack.
You will feel cool air rushing in.
This is wind.

The sun warms the water in oceans, lakes, and rivers.
Some of the water mixes with warm air as mist.
This is water vapor.
The warm water vapor rises.
When water changes into water vapor,
we say that it *evaporates*.

Warm water evaporates faster than cold water.
On a hot day a great deal of water vapor
mixes with the warm air over the water.
When warm air with water vapor meets cool air,
the warm air is pushed up.
It rises high above the earth,
where it is always cold.
The warm air gets cooler and cooler
as it rises.
As it gets cooler,
the water vapor in the air
changes back into drops of water.
It *condenses*.

Millions and millions of tiny water drops
condense from the cooled water vapor.
As these drops of water come together
they form clouds.
Soon large, dark clouds are in the sky.

Have you ever noticed drops of water
which form on the bathroom mirror during a bath?
The warm air in the bathroom
is filled with water vapor.
It is cooled when it touches the cold mirror.
The water vapor condenses into drops of water.

The same kind of thing happens outdoors.
Up in the air,
the drops get bigger and bigger
as more water vapor condenses.
Soon the air cannot hold the big drops
which make the clouds.
The drops begin to fall as rain.

Now we have a thunderstorm.
Up in the dark storm clouds,
high winds are blowing.
The strong winds sweep up some of the raindrops.
Over and over again the raindrops start to fall.

Over and over again some of the drops
are blown up into the storm cloud.
Electricity begins to build up in the drops of water.
Nobody knows exactly how this happens.
But each drop gets more and more electricity.
The electricity tries to escape.
At last it finds a way.

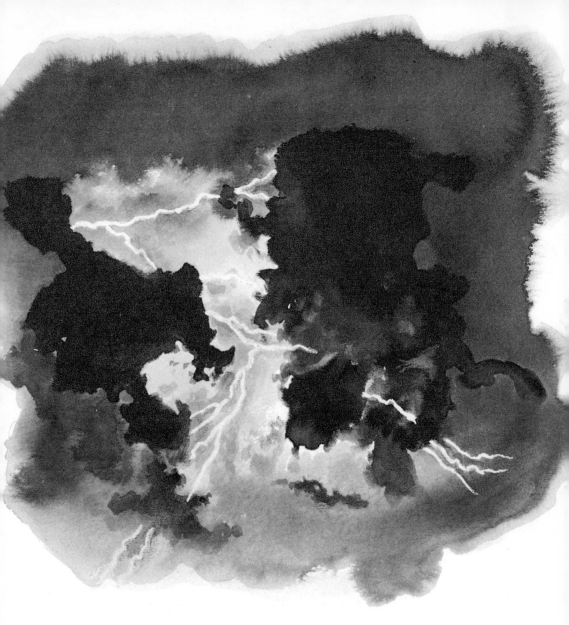

A huge spark of electricity
jumps between the storm cloud and earth
or between one storm cloud and another.
This spark of electricity is lightning.

You can build up a small amount, or *charge*,
of electricity in your body.
Rub your shoe back and forth on a rug.
Then touch a metal doorknob.
You will feel a small electrical shock
as the electricity goes from your body to the metal.

On a cold, dry day you might see a tiny spark
jump from your hand to the doorknob
just before you touch it.
The spark is the electricity
jumping from your body to the knob.

Lightning carries a very powerful charge of electricity.
This electricity immediately heats anything
which it strikes.
Things that are heated *expand*, or get bigger.

When lightning flashes through the air,
it heats the air.
The air spreads out suddenly.
It makes a loud *bang!*
It is the same as sticking a pin into a blown-up balloon.
Whenever air moves out all at once,
it makes a loud noise.
The sound of the rush of air
after lightning is thunder.

It is best to be indoors during a storm,
because lightning can be dangerous.
Lightning can cause a burn or an electric shock.
If lightning strikes a tree or a wooden building,
it can start a fire or an explosion.

The safest place during a storm
is in a building with a metal frame
or in a car.
If lightning strikes the building or the car,
the metal frame carries the electricity safely
into the ground.

During a storm
never take shelter under a tall tree
or under a tree that is standing alone.
Tall objects can be targets for lightning.
Keep away from the water during a storm.
Water attracts lightning.

Wooden buildings that are taller
than nearby houses or trees
often have a metal rod sticking up from the roof.
This is a lightning rod.
The lightning is attracted to the higher rod.
From the rod the electricity passes
through a wire into the earth.

Not all storms are thunder and lightning storms.
Sometimes the upward winds of a storm are so powerful
that they blow the raindrops
two or three miles up into the air.
It is so cold there
that the drops form into balls of ice,
called hailstones.
The hailstones start to fall.
They get covered with water,
and some are then blown up again.
More ice forms on the hailstones.
This happens over and over again.

When the hailstones are covered with many coats of ice, they fall to earth in a hailstorm.
Once in a while, hailstones get as large as baseballs.

Thunderstorms and hailstorms usually happen
during the spring and summer.

But there are other storms
that may happen during winter.
If rain falls during very cold weather,
the drops may freeze.
Frozen drops of rain are called sleet.
When they fall, we have a sleet storm.

Sometimes it is too cold
for the water vapor to change back into water.
Raindrops do not form.
Instead, the water vapor itself freezes
and becomes snowflakes.
This makes a snowstorm.
A snowstorm with very strong, cold winds is a blizzard

There are also storms
in which the wind spins and whirls about.

Tornadoes,

hurricanes,

and typhoons are storms

with very fast, very strong whirling winds.

Storms are important to all of us.
They are *most* important
to airplane pilots, sailors, and farmers.

They have to know all about storms.
They know
when a storm is coming,
what causes thunder and lightning,
and how to be safe during a storm.

Do you?

The Author

MELVIN BERGER lives in Great Neck, New York, with his family. He teaches science in the Plainview public schools.

A graduate of the University of Rochester, he did graduate work at Teachers College, Columbia University, and at the University of London in England.

Mr. Berger is the author of *Atoms* and *Gravity* in this series, as well as a number of books for children and scientific articles for magazine publication.

The Artist

JOSEPH CELLINI lives in New Jersey with his wife, who is also an artist.

Mr. Cellini has illustrated many books for boys and girls, a number of them science subjects in a variety of areas.

The *Science Is What and Why* Books

An introduction to the physical and natural sciences for the primary school child. To be read to or to read to himself. An approach planned to broaden conceptual awareness about

YOU,

YOU AND YOUR EARTH,

and *YOU AND YOUR UNIVERSE*

During every active minute of his life, a child learns: through his own experiences, while exploring interests with his peers, and by communication through media and books.

Each subject in the series presents knowledge that a child can relate to his own experiences, gives information that can be examined and tested with others and stimulates further investigation.

YOU

Machines help you work

LEVERS

WHEELS

TELEPHONES

YOU AND YOUR EARTH

CONSERVATION AND ECOLOGY

What the earth gives to us and what we give to the earth

·RAIN AND THE VALLEY

THIS IS THE FOREST

WHO WILL WASH THE RIVER?

ENVIRONMENT

The earth is always changing

GLACIERS

ROCK ALL AROUND

TIDES

SEASONS

SEASHELL TOWNS

STORMS

YOU AND YOUR UNIVERSE

Forces that make things happen

LIGHT

SOUND

ECHOES

GRAVITY

MOTION

Forces that can make power

ELECTRICITY

MAGNETS

HEAT

FRICTION

ATOMS